THE SECRETS OF COOKING SOLO

Unlock a World of Delicious Possibilities!

By: CAROLINE E. COOPER

Caroline E. Cooper

Introduction..4

CHAPTER ONE..7

Basic Kitchen Supplies..7

CHAPTER TWO...10

Kitchen Utensils..10

CHAPTER THREE...13

Cookware..13

20 COOKWARES AND HOW THEY'RE USED..........................14

CHAPTER FOUR: RECIPES..17

Breakfast..17

Lunch...35

Dinner...46

Snacks...63

Desserts..73

CHAPTER FIVE..88

Meal Planning..88

CHAPTER SIX...91

Healthy Eating Tips..91

CHAPTER SEVEN..95

Food Safety..95

CHAPTER EIGHT..99

Cooking Methods..99

CHAPTER NINE...103

Cooking Tips..103

Conclusion...106

Introduction

Cooking for one can be a daunting task. It's easy to feel overwhelmed when it comes to making meals for one person, but solo cooking can be incredibly rewarding. With a little bit of creativity, cooking for yourself can be an enjoyable and satisfying experience. Not only that, but it's a great way to learn new recipes and develop your cooking skills.

Solo cooking offers a number of benefits, from the convenience of being able to make meals for yourself whenever you want to the joys of being able to experiment with different ingredients and recipes. It's also a great way to save money, since you don't have to worry about buying too much food or wasting it. And of course, it's an opportunity to get creative in the kitchen and have some fun.

Whether you're a novice or a seasoned cook, solo cooking can be a great way to explore your culinary talents. With the right ingredients and tools, you can create delicious, healthy, and affordable meals in no time. From simple one-pot dishes to complex multi-course meals, there's something for everyone.

So, if you're feeling a little daunted by the thought of solo cooking, take a deep breath, put on your apron, and get ready to explore the world of solo cooking!

Cooking for yourself is a great pleasure because it allows you to express yourself in a creative and delicious way. There is something special about making a meal from scratch and taking the time to make something for yourself. It can help you to relax and feel more in control of your own life, as you are in charge of what you are eating. It also gives you the opportunity to explore different flavors and recipes and to learn about nutrition.

Cooking for yourself can also be very rewarding, as you feel a sense of accomplishment from creating a tasty meal. You also get to enjoy the fruits of your labour, which can be especially satisfying.

Finally, cooking for yourself can be a great way to save money. By buying ingredients in bulk and making meals with them, you can save a significant amount of money that you would otherwise spend on ready-made meals.

Cooking for yourself can be an incredibly fulfilling activity and can provide you with both physical and mental benefits. It is a great way to express yourself, save money, and enjoy the process of creating something delicious.

As you cook your dish. The first step is to gather the ingredients you need. Once you have all the ingredients, you can start to prepare them. This may include chopping, slicing, dicing, and marinating. Once all the ingredients are prepped, you can start cooking. Depending on the dish, you may need to simmer, saute, or bake. Once the dish is cooked, you can season it with herbs and spices as desired, and serve it to your guests. Enjoy!

Happy cooking!

CHAPTER ONE
Basic Kitchen Supplies

1. Knife: used to cut, chop, and mince food.

2. Cutting Board: a flat surface used to cut food.

3. Pot: used to boil, simmer, and cook food.

4. Pan: used to fry, sauté, and roast food.

5. Spatula: used to stir, flip, and scrape food.

6. Ladle: used to scoop and serve liquids.

7. Whisk: used to mix ingredients together.

8. Measuring Cup: used to measure ingredients.

9. Measuring Spoon: used to measure small amounts of ingredients.

10. Colander: used to strain food.

11. Can Opener: used to open canned food.

12. Peeler: used to peel vegetables and fruits.

13. Grater: used to grate food.

14. Blender: used to blend ingredients together.

15. Mixer: used to mix ingredients together.

16. Dish Towel: used to dry dishes and clean up spills.

17. Apron: used to protect clothing from splashes and

spills.

18. Oven Mitt: used to protect hands from hot ovens and surfaces.

19. Kitchen Towel: used to wipe counters and tables.

20. Sponges: used to scrub dishes, pans, and surfaces.

Knives are essential to cutting, chopping, and mincing food. Cutting boards provide a flat surface to work on while cutting. Pots and pans are used to boil, simmer, fry, sauté, and roast food. Spatulas are used to stir, flip, and scrape food. A ladle is used to scoop and serve liquids. A whisk is used to mix ingredients together. Ingredients are measured using measuring cups and spoons. Food is strained using a colander. Can openers are used to open cans of food. Peeling vegetables and fruits is done using a peeler. To shred food, a grater is used. A blender is used to combine components.. A mixer is used to mix ingredients together. Dish towels are used to dry dishes and clean up spills. Aprons are used to protect clothing from splashes and spills. Oven mitts are used to protect hands from hot ovens and surfaces. Kitchen towels are used to wipe counters and tables. Sponges are used to scrub dishes, pans, and surfaces. With these basic kitchen supplies, you can create delicious meals in no time!

Basic Kitchen Supplies, such as knives, cutting boards, pans, and spatulas, are being used on a daily basis to prepare meals for families, and to create delicious recipes. They can be used to chop, dice, and mince vegetables, as well as to sauté, stir-fry, and bake dishes. Pots and pans can be used for boiling, steaming, and simmering, and baking dishes can be used for creating cakes and other desserts. Additionally, the Basic Kitchen Supplies can also be used for cleaning up after meals, as kitchen sponges, cloths, and scrubbers can be used to quickly and efficiently clean up any mess that may have been created during the cooking process.

Overall, the Basic Kitchen Supplies are essential for creating tasty meals, as well as keeping any kitchen space organized and clean. They are the backbone of any kitchen, and without them, preparing meals can be a difficult and time-consuming process.

CHAPTER TWO

Kitchen Utensils

Kitchen utensils are an integral part of any kitchen. They are used for a wide range of activities, from cooking to food preparation and serving. Kitchen utensils can be divided into two main categories: those used for cooking and those used for food preparation.

Cooking utensils include pots, pans, skillets, colanders, strainers, graters, sieves, whisks, spatulas, ladles, tongs, rolling pins, and other tools used for stirring, flipping, folding, and mixing ingredients. Pots and pans are essential in any kitchen and come in a variety of materials, such as stainless steel, aluminum, copper, and cast iron. Skillets are used to fry food, while colanders, strainers, and sieves are used to drain and strain liquids. Graters, sieves, and whisks are used to break down ingredients, such as cheese and spices, into smaller pieces. Spatulas are used for stirring and flipping, while ladles and tongs are used for serving food. Rolling pins are used for rolling dough or flattening food.

Food preparation utensils are used for slicing, dicing, chopping, and mixing ingredients. They include knives, cutting boards, graters, peelers, blenders, food processors, and mixers. Knives come in a variety of sizes and shapes, such as paring knives, chef's knives, and cleavers, and are used for cutting and slicing food. Cutting boards are essential for any kitchen and come in a variety of materials, such as wood, plastic, and marble. Graters, peelers, and zesters are used to break down ingredients into smaller pieces, while blenders and food processors are used to blend and puree ingredients. Mixers are used to combine wet and dry ingredients.

Kitchen utensils are also used for serving food. They include plates, bowls, cups, glasses, trays, platters, and utensils, such as forks, spoons, and knives. Plates, bowls, and cups come in a variety of materials and sizes and are used to hold and serve food. Glasses and mugs are used for beverages. Trays and platters are used for presentation and serving. Utensils, such as forks, spoons, and knives, are used for eating and serving food.

Kitchen utensils can be made from a variety of materials, such as stainless steel, plastic, wood, and ceramic. Stainless steel is the most common material used for kitchen utensils, as it is durable, easy to clean, and heat-resistant. Plastic is lightweight and inexpensive, but can be easily scratched and is not as durable as stainless steel. Wood is attractive and can be used to make decorative utensils, but it is prone to staining and can easily be scratched or marked. Ceramic is non-porous, which makes it easy to clean and resistant to bacteria.

In conclusion, kitchen utensils are an essential part of any kitchen. They are used for a wide range of activities, from cooking to food preparation and serving. Kitchen utensils come in a variety of materials, such as stainless steel, plastic, wood, and ceramic. They are easy to use and can help to create a variety of dishes. With the right utensils, any kitchen can be transformed into a culinary masterpiece.

CHAPTER THREE

Cookware

Cookware typically consists of pots, pans, skillets, woks, roasting pans, and baking dishes. Other common cookware items include strainers, colanders, graters, griddles, egg poachers, and steamers. Cookware can be made from various materials such as stainless steel, copper, aluminum, cast iron, glass, and non-stick coatings. The importance of cookware in the kitchen cannot be overstated. Good quality cookware can help to make cooking easier, faster, and more enjoyable. Additionally, having the right cookware helps to ensure that food is cooked properly and evenly. In addition to convenience, cookware can help to save time and energy in the kitchen. With the right cookware, it is easy to cook food quickly and consistently. Using the right cookware can also help to make meals healthier. Many types of cookware contain non-stick coatings that help to reduce the amount of oil, butter, and fat that is used in cooking. Non-stick coatings also help to prevent food from sticking and burning, which can reduce the amount of time and energy needed to cook meals. Cookware can also be used to add flavor and texture to a meal. Cast iron cookware is known for its ability to evenly heat and retain heat, which can help to create flavorful meals. The same is true for copper cookware. Copper is an excellent conductor of heat, which makes it ideal for cooking delicate items like fish and vegetables that need to be cooked quickly and evenly.

Cookware can help you cook delicious and healthy meals for yourself and your family. It can help you save time and money by allowing you to cook more efficiently. It can also help you create meals that are more flavorful and healthier, since you can control the ingredients used. Finally, cookware can help you make the most of the ingredients you have on hand, as you can use different pieces of cookware for different types of cooking.

20 COOKWARES AND HOW THEY'RE USED

1. Saucepan: Used to cook sauces and soups.

2. Frying pan: Used to fry foods such as eggs, pancakes and vegetables.

3. Wok: Used to stir-fry vegetables, meats, and other ingredients.

4. Dutch oven: Used to braise and stew meats and vegetables.

5. Stockpot: Used to make stocks, soups, and other liquid dishes.

6. Roasting pan: Used to roast meats and vegetables in the oven.

7. Griddle: Used to cook pancakes, eggs, and other flat foods.

8. Baking dish: Used to bake casseroles and other dishes.

9. Casserole dish: Used to bake and serve casseroles.

10. Skillet: Used to sauté and sear meats, vegetables, and other ingredients.

11. Baking sheet: Used to bake cookies, pastries, and other baked goods.

12. Gratin dish: Used to bake and serve gratins.

13. Steamer: Used to steam vegetables, seafood, and other foods.

14. Double boiler: Used to melt chocolate, heat sauces, and cook delicate foods.

15. Rice cooker: Used to cook perfect rice every time.

16. Pressure cooker: Used to quickly cook food under pressure.

17. Deep fryer: Used to deep fry foods such as french fries and donuts.

18. Saute pan: Used to sauté meats and vegetables.

19. Waffle iron: Used to make perfect waffles every time.

20. Crock pot: Used to slowly cook meats, stews, and soups.

CHAPTER FOUR: RECIPES
Breakfast

EAT A PROPER BREAKFAST

A proper breakfast might include whole grains, protein, and a serving of fruit. Some ideas include oatmeal with nuts and a banana, scrambled eggs with whole wheat toast and a glass of orange juice, or a smoothie with Greek yogurt, berries, and chia seeds.

It is important to make sure your breakfast is balanced and contains all the nutrients you need to start your day. A balanced breakfast should include complex carbohydrates, protein, and healthy fats. This helps keep your energy levels steady throughout the day and helps you maintain a healthy weight.

20 Breakfast recipes with ingredients and Instruction with Prep Time

1. Overnight Oats

Ingredients:

1/2 cup old-fashioned oats,

1/2 cup milk,

1/2 teaspoon ground cinnamon,

1/4 teaspoon ground nutmeg,

1 tablespoon honey or maple syrup,

1/4 cup of your favorite dried fruit,

1/4 cup of your favorite nuts,

1 teaspoon of your favorite nut butter

Instructions: In a bowl, mix together oats, milk, cinnamon, nutmeg, and honey or maple syrup. Cover and refrigerate overnight. In the morning, add in dried fruit, nuts, and nut butter. Mix together and enjoy.

Prep Time: 5 minutes + overnight

2. Avocado Toast

Ingredients:

2 slices of your favorite bread,

1/4 avocado,

1 teaspoon olive oil,

1/4 teaspoon garlic powder,

salt and pepper to taste

Instructions:

Toast the bread and spread avocado on top. Drizzle olive oil over avocado, then sprinkle with garlic powder, salt and pepper. Enjoy.

Prep Time: 5 minutes

3. Banana Pancakes

Ingredients:

1 cup all-purpose flour,

1 tablespoon baking powder,

1 teaspoon salt,

1 tablespoon sugar,

1 cup milk,

1 egg,

1 banana,

2 tablespoons butter

Instructions:

In a bowl, mix together flour, baking powder, salt and sugar. In a separate bowl, mix together milk, egg, banana, and butter. Add wet ingredients to dry ingredients and mix until just combined. Heat a skillet over medium heat and grease with butter. Drop 1/4 cup of batter onto the skillet, cook for about 2 minutes then flip and cook for an additional 2 minutes. Repeat with remaining batter.

Prep Time: 10 minutes

4. Yogurt Parfait

Ingredients:

1/2 cup plain Greek yogurt,

1/4 cup granola,

1/4 cup fresh berries

Instructions:

In a bowl, layer the yogurt, granola, and berries. Enjoy.

Prep Time: 5 minutes

5. Egg and Cheese Sandwich

Ingredients:

2 slices of your favorite bread,

1 teaspoon butter,

1 egg, 1 slice of cheddar cheese

Instructions:

Heat a skillet over medium heat and grease with butter. Crack the egg into the skillet and cook until the egg whites are set. Place the cheese on top of the egg and cook until the cheese melts. Assemble the egg and cheese between the 2 slices of bread. Enjoy.

Prep Time: 5 minutes

6. Smoothie Bowl

Ingredients:

1/2 cup frozen mango,

 1/2 cup frozen strawberries,

1/2 cup almond milk,

1/4 cup granola,

1 tablespoon chia seeds

Instructions:

Blend together the mango, strawberries, and almond milk until smooth. Pour into a bowl and top with granola and chia seeds. Enjoy.

Prep Time: 5 minutes

7. Egg Muffins

Ingredients:

6 eggs,

1/4 cup diced bell pepper,

1/4 cup diced onion,

1/4 cup diced ham,

1/4 cup shredded cheddar cheese, salt and pepper to taste

Instructions:

Preheat oven to 350°F. Grease a muffin tin with cooking spray. In a large bowl, whisk together the eggs. Add in bell pepper, onion, ham, and cheese. Season with salt and pepper. Divide the mixture evenly between the muffin tins. Bake for 15-20 minutes, or until the eggs are set. Enjoy.

Prep Time: 10 minutes

8. Fruit and Nut Granola

Ingredients:

2 cups rolled oats,

1/4 cup honey,

1/4 cup melted coconut oil,

1/2 teaspoon ground cinnamon,

1/2 teaspoon ground nutmeg,

1/4 cup chopped nuts,

 1/4 cup of your favorite dried fruit.

Instructions:

Preheat oven to 350°F. In a large bowl, mix together oats, honey, coconut oil, cinnamon and nutmeg. Spread the mixture onto a baking sheet and bake for 20 minutes, stirring occasionally. Remove from the oven and mix in nuts and dried fruit. Allow to cool before storing. Enjoy.

Prep Time: 10 minutes

9. French Toast

Ingredients:

2 slices of your favorite bread,

2 eggs,

 1/4 cup milk,

1 teaspoon ground cinnamon,

1 teaspoon vanilla extract,

butter for cooking

Instructions:

In a shallow bowl, mix together eggs, milk, cinnamon and vanilla extract. Dip the bread slices into the egg mixture and allow them to soak for a few minutes. Heat a skillet over medium heat and grease with butter. Cook the French toast for about 2 minutes on each side, until golden brown. Enjoy.

Prep Time: 10 minutes

10. Omelette

Ingredients:

2 eggs,

1/4 cup diced bell pepper,

1/4 cup diced ham,

1/4 cup shredded cheddar cheese,

salt and pepper to taste

Instructions: Heat a skillet over medium heat and grease with butter. In a bowl, whisk together the eggs. Add bell pepper, ham and cheese. Pour the egg mixture into the skillet and cook for about 2 minutes. Using a spatula, fold the omelette in half and cook for an additional 2 minutes. Enjoy.

Prep Time: 10 minutes

11. Savory Oatmeal

Ingredients:

1/2 cup rolled oats,

1 cup vegetable broth,

1/4 cup diced onion,

1/4 cup diced bell pepper,

1/4 cup diced mushrooms,

1 tablespoon olive oil, salt and pepper to taste

Instructions:

Heat a skillet over medium heat and add in olive oil. Add onion, bell pepper and mushrooms and cook for 2-3 minutes. Add in oats and vegetable broth and bring to a boil. Cook for about 5 minutes, stirring occasionally. Season with salt and pepper. Enjoy.

Prep Time: 10 minutes

12. Protein Shake

Ingredients:

1/2 cup almond milk,

1 scoop protein powder,

1 banana, 1 tablespoon peanut butter,

1 teaspoon ground flaxseed

Instructions:

In a blender, combine almond milk, protein powder, banana, peanut butter, and flaxseed. Blend until smooth. Enjoy.

Prep Time: 5 minutes

13. Egg Salad Sandwich

Ingredients:

4 boiled eggs,

1 teaspoon mustard,

1 teaspoon mayonnaise,

1/4 cup diced celery,

1/4 cup diced bell pepper,

1 teaspoon diced red onion,

salt and pepper to taste

Instructions:

Peel and mash the boiled eggs. In a bowl, mix together the mashed eggs, mustard, mayonnaise, celery, bell pepper, and red onion. Season with salt and pepper. Spread the egg salad onto your favorite bread and enjoy.

Prep Time: 10 minutes

14. Coconut Steel Cut Oats

Ingredients:

1/2 cup steel cut oats,

1 cup coconut milk,

1 teaspoon ground cinnamon,

2 tablespoons honey,

1/4 cup shredded coconut

Instructions:

In a saucepan, bring the oats, coconut milk, and cinnamon to a boil. Reduce heat to low and cook for about 10 minutes, stirring occasionally. Remove from heat and stir in honey and shredded coconut. Enjoy.

Prep Time: 10 minutes

15. Baked Sweet Potato

Ingredients:

1 sweet potato,

1 teaspoon olive oil,

1/4 teaspoon garlic powder,

salt and pepper to taste

Instructions:

Preheat oven to 375°F. Pierce the sweet potato a few times with a fork. Rub the sweet potato with olive oil and garlic powder, then season with salt and pepper. Place on a baking sheet and bake for 45 minutes, or until the potato is soft. Enjoy.

Prep Time: 5 minutes

16. Cottage Cheese Toast

Ingredients:

2 slices of your favorite bread,

1/4 cup cottage cheese,

1/4 cup diced tomatoes,

1/4 teaspoon garlic powder,

salt and pepper to taste

Instructions:

Toast the bread and spread cottage cheese on top. Top with tomatoes, garlic powder, salt and pepper. Enjoy.

Prep Time: 5 minutes

17. Quinoa Bowl

Ingredients:

1/2 cup cooked quinoa,

1/4 cup diced bell pepper,

1/4 cup diced red onion,

1/4 cup corn, 1/2 avocado,

1 tablespoon olive oil,

 1 teaspoon lime juice

Instructions:

In a bowl, mix together cooked quinoa, bell pepper, red onion, and corn. Top with avocado, olive oil, and lime juice. Enjoy.

Prep Time: 10 minutes

18. Spinach and Feta Egg Wrap

Ingredients:

2 eggs, 1/4 cup spinach,

1 tablespoon feta cheese,

 1 whole-wheat wrap,

salt and pepper to taste

Instructions:

Heat a skillet over medium heat and grease with butter. Crack the eggs into the skillet and cook until the egg whites are set. Add in the spinach and feta cheese and cook for an additional 1-2 minutes. Place the egg mixture onto the wrap and season with salt and pepper. Enjoy.

Prep Time: 10 minutes

19. Oatmeal with Fruit

Ingredients:

1/2 cup old-fashioned oats,

1 cup milk,

1/4 teaspoon ground cinnamon,

1/4 cup chopped almonds,

1/4 cup of your favorite dried fruit

Instructions:

In a saucepan, bring the oats, milk, and cinnamon to a boil. Reduce heat to low and cook for about 5 minutes, stirring occasionally. Remove from heat and stir in almonds and dried fruit. Enjoy.

Prep Time: 10 minutes

20. Baked Egg Avocado

Ingredients:

1/2 avocado,

1 egg,

1 tablespoon shredded cheddar cheese,

salt and pepper to taste

Instructions:

Preheat oven to 425°F. Slice the avocado in half and remove the pit. Crack the egg into the center of the avocado and top with cheddar cheese and salt and pepper. Place the avocado halves on a baking sheet and bake for 15 minutes. Enjoy.

Prep Time: 5 minutes

Lunch
10 Lunch recipes with ingredients and Instruction with Prep Time

1. Mediterranean Quinoa Bowl – Prep Time: 10 minutes

Ingredients:

-1 cup cooked quinoa

-1/4 cup cucumber, diced

-1/4 cup cherry tomatoes, halved

-1/4 cup feta cheese crumbles

-1/4 cup kalamata olives, sliced

-1/4 cup fresh parsley, chopped

-2 tablespoons extra virgin olive oil

-1 tablespoon red wine vinegar

-1/2 teaspoon garlic powder

-Salt and pepper to taste

Instructions:

In a medium bowl, combine cooked quinoa, cucumber, tomatoes, feta, olives, and parsley. In a small bowl, whisk together olive oil, red wine vinegar, garlic powder, salt, and pepper. Drizzle dressing over the quinoa bowl and toss to combine. Serve chilled or at room temperature.

2. Baked Salmon with Lemon-Dill Sauce – Prep Time: 20 minutes

Ingredients:

-1 pound salmon fillet

-1 tablespoon olive oil

-Salt and pepper to taste

-2 tablespoons butter

-2 tablespoons all-purpose flour

-1 cup chicken broth

-2 tablespoons fresh lemon juice

-2 tablespoons chopped fresh dill

-2 tablespoons chopped fresh parsley

Instructions:

 Preheat oven to 375°F. Place salmon fillet on a baking sheet lined with parchment paper. Brush salmon with olive oil and season with salt and pepper. Bake for 12-15 minutes, or until cooked through. Meanwhile, melt butter in a medium saucepan over medium heat. Whisk in flour and cook for 1 minute. Slowly whisk in chicken broth and lemon juice, stirring constantly until the sauce begins to thicken. Stir in dill and parsley. Remove from heat and season with salt and pepper. Serve salmon with lemon-dill sauce.

3. Greek Yogurt Chicken Salad – Prep Time: 10 minutes

Ingredients:

-2 cups cooked chicken, diced

-1/2 cup plain Greek yogurt

-2 tablespoons mayonnaise

-2 tablespoons diced red onion

-2 tablespoons diced celery

-2 tablespoons diced dill pickles

-1 tablespoon fresh lemon juice

-1 tablespoon chopped fresh dill

-Salt and pepper to taste

Instructions:

In a medium bowl, combine chicken, yogurt, mayonnaise, red onion, celery, pickles, lemon juice, and dill. Season with salt and pepper. Serve with crackers or on a bed of lettuce.

4. Avocado Egg Toast – Prep Time: 5 minutes

Ingredients:

-2 slices whole grain bread

-2 eggs

-1/2 avocado, sliced

-Salt and pepper to taste

Instructions:

Toast bread slices in a toaster or under the broiler. Fry eggs in a skillet over medium heat. Top toast slices with fried eggs and avocado slices. Season with salt and pepper.

5. Baked Sweet Potato and Black Bean Burritos – Prep Time: 25 minutes

Ingredients:

-4 whole wheat tortillas

-1 cup cooked black beans

-1 cup cooked sweet potato, mashed

-1/4 cup diced red onion

-1/4 cup diced bell pepper

-1/4 cup chopped fresh cilantro

-1/2 cup shredded cheese

-1/4 cup salsa

Instructions:

Preheat oven to 375°F. In a medium bowl, combine black beans, mashed sweet potato, red onion, bell pepper, cilantro, and cheese. Divide mixture between tortillas and roll into burritos. Place burritos on a baking sheet lined with parchment paper. Bake for 15 minutes. Serve with salsa.

6. Turkey Lettuce Wraps – Prep Time: 10 minutes

Ingredients:

-1/2 pound ground turkey

-1/2 teaspoon garlic powder

-1/2 teaspoon onion powder

-1/2 teaspoon cumin

-1/4 teaspoon chili powder

-Salt and pepper to taste

-1/4 cup diced red onion

-1/4 cup diced bell pepper

-1/4 cup diced tomatoes

-4 butter lettuce leaves

Instructions:

In a medium skillet over medium heat, cook turkey with garlic powder, onion powder, cumin, chili powder, salt, and pepper. When turkey is cooked through, add red onion, bell pepper, and tomatoes. Cook for 2-3 minutes, or until vegetables are tender. Divide turkey mixture among lettuce leaves and serve.

7. Egg and Spinach Salad – Prep Time: 10 minutes

Ingredients:

-3 cups baby spinach

-3 hard-boiled eggs, chopped

-1/4 cup diced red onion

-1/4 cup diced tomato

-1/4 cup crumbled feta cheese

-2 tablespoons extra virgin olive oil

-2 tablespoons balsamic vinegar

-Salt and pepper to taste

Instructions:

In a large bowl, combine spinach, eggs, red onion, tomato, and feta cheese. In a small bowl, whisk together olive oil, balsamic vinegar, salt, and pepper. Drizzle dressing over the salad and toss to combine. Serve chilled.

8. Slow Cooker Chicken Fajitas – Prep Time: 10 minutes

Ingredients:

-1 pound boneless skinless chicken breasts

-1 red bell pepper, sliced

-1 green bell pepper, sliced

-1 onion, sliced

-1 tablespoon chili powder

-1 teaspoon garlic powder

-1 teaspoon cumin

-1/2 teaspoon paprika

-1/2 teaspoon dried oregano

-1/2 teaspoon salt

-1/4 teaspoon black pepper

-1/4 cup chicken broth

-8 flour tortillas

Instructions:

Place chicken, bell peppers, onion, chili powder, garlic powder, cumin, paprika, oregano, salt, pepper, and chicken broth in a slow cooker. Stir to combine. Cook on low for 6-7 hours, or on high for 3-4 hours. Serve chicken mixture in flour tortillas.

9. Zucchini Noodles with Pesto – Prep Time: 10 minutes

Ingredients:

-2 zucchinis, spiralized

-1/4 cup basil pesto

-1/4 cup cherry tomatoes, halved

-1/4 cup shredded Parmesan cheese

-2 tablespoons toasted pine nuts

Instructions:

Place zucchini noodles in a large bowl. Add pesto and toss to combine. Divide among two plates and top with tomatoes, Parmesan cheese, and pine nuts. Serve chilled.

10. Mexican Rice Bowl – Prep Time: 15 minutes

Ingredients:

-1 cup cooked white rice

-1/2 cup black beans, cooked

-1/4 cup corn

-1/4 cup diced tomatoes

-1/4 cup diced red onion

-2 tablespoons chopped fresh cilantro

-2 tablespoons extra virgin olive oil

-1 teaspoon lime juice

-1/2 teaspoon chili powder

-Salt and pepper to taste

Instructions:

In a medium bowl, combine cooked rice, black beans, corn, tomatoes, red onion, and cilantro. In a small bowl, whisk together olive oil, lime juice, chili powder, salt, and pepper. Drizzle dressing over the rice bowl and toss to combine. Serve chilled or at room temperature.

Dinner
10 dinner recipes with ingredients and instructions
with prep time

1. Grilled Salmon with Asparagus and Quinoa:

Ingredients:

- 4 (4 oz.) salmon fillets

- 2 tablespoons olive oil

- ½ teaspoon salt

- ½ teaspoon ground black pepper

- 1 bunch asparagus, trimmed

- 1 cup cooked quinoa

Instructions:

- Preheat a grill over medium-high heat.

- Brush salmon fillets with olive oil and season with salt and pepper.

- Place on the grill and cook for 4 minutes per side, until cooked through.

- Toss asparagus with olive oil and season with salt and pepper.

- Grill asparagus for 3 minutes per side, until tender.

- Serve salmon and asparagus with cooked quinoa.

Prep Time: 15 minutes

2. Roasted Vegetable Bowls with Tofu:

Ingredients:

- 1 block extra-firm tofu

- 1 tablespoon olive oil

- 1 teaspoon garlic powder

- 1 teaspoon paprika

- 1 teaspoon onion powder

- 1 teaspoon Italian seasoning

- ½ teaspoon salt

- ½ teaspoon ground black pepper

- 1 red bell pepper, chopped

- 1 yellow bell pepper, chopped

- 1 zucchini, chopped

- 1 red onion, chopped

- 2 cloves garlic, minced

- 2 tablespoons balsamic vinegar

Instructions:

- Preheat oven to 400°F.

- Drain tofu and cut into cubes.

- In a large bowl, combine tofu, olive oil, garlic powder, paprika, onion powder, Italian seasoning, salt, and pepper.

- Toss until tofu is well-coated.

- Spread on a baking sheet and bake for 25 minutes, stirring once halfway through.

- Meanwhile, in a large bowl, combine bell peppers, zucchini, red onion, garlic, balsamic vinegar, and remaining olive oil.

- Toss until vegetables are well-coated.

- Spread on a separate baking sheet and bake for 20 minutes, stirring once halfway through.

- Serve tofu and vegetables in bowls.

Prep Time: 25 minutes

3. Quinoa Burrito Bowls:

Ingredients:

- 1 cup uncooked quinoa

- 2 cups vegetable broth

- 1 tablespoon olive oil

- 1 red bell pepper, chopped

- 1 green bell pepper, chopped

- 1 yellow onion, chopped

- 2 cloves garlic, minced

- 1 can black beans, drained and rinsed

- 2 teaspoons chili powder

- 1 teaspoon ground cumin

- ½ teaspoon salt

- ½ teaspoon ground black pepper

- 1 cup corn

- 1 avocado, diced

- 2 tablespoons lime juice

- 2 tablespoons chopped fresh cilantro

Instructions:

- In a medium saucepan, combine quinoa and vegetable broth. Bring to a boil. Reduce heat to low, cover, and simmer for 15 minutes.

- Meanwhile, heat olive oil in a large skillet over medium heat.

- Add bell peppers, onion, and garlic and cook for 5 minutes, stirring occasionally.

- Add black beans, chili powder, cumin, salt, and pepper and cook for 5 minutes, stirring occasionally.

- Add corn and cook for 5 minutes, stirring occasionally.

- In a small bowl, combine avocado, lime juice, and cilantro. Set aside.

- Serve quinoa in bowls topped with vegetables and avocado mixture.

Prep Time: 25 minutes

4. Broccoli and Cheese Stuffed Chicken Breast:

Ingredients:

- 4 (4 oz.) boneless, skinless chicken breasts

- 1 tablespoon olive oil

- ½ teaspoon salt

- ½ teaspoon ground black pepper

- 2 cups broccoli florets

- ¼ cup grated Parmesan cheese

- ¼ cup shredded mozzarella cheese

- 1 tablespoon chopped fresh parsley

Instructions:

- Preheat oven to 375°F.

- Heat olive oil in a large skillet over medium heat.

- Season chicken breasts with salt and pepper and cook for 5 minutes per side, until cooked through.

- Meanwhile, steam broccoli until tender.

- In a medium bowl, combine broccoli, Parmesan cheese, mozzarella cheese, and parsley.

- Spoon mixture onto chicken breasts and fold over to enclose.

- Place stuffed chicken breasts in an oven-safe baking dish.

- Bake for 15 minutes, until cheese is melted and chicken is cooked through.

Caroline E. Cooper

Prep Time: 25 minutes

5. Cauliflower Fried Rice:

Ingredients:

- 1 head cauliflower, grated

- 2 tablespoons olive oil

- 1 cup diced onion

- 1 cup diced carrots

- 1 cup frozen peas

- 2 cloves garlic, minced

- 3 eggs, lightly beaten

- 2 tablespoons low-sodium soy sauce

Instructions:

- Heat olive oil in a large skillet over medium heat.

- Add onion, carrots, peas, and garlic and cook for 5 minutes, stirring occasionally.

- Add cauliflower and cook for 5 minutes, stirring occasionally.

- Push vegetables to the sides of the skillet and add eggs.

- Cook for 2 minutes, stirring occasionally.

- Stir in soy sauce and cook for 2 minutes, stirring occasionally.

- Serve warm.

Prep Time: 15 minutes

6. Baked Sweet Potato with Chickpeas and Spinach:

Ingredients:

- 2 sweet potatoes

- 2 tablespoons olive oil

- ½ teaspoon salt

- ½ teaspoon ground black pepper

- 1 (15 oz.) can chickpeas, drained and rinsed

- 1 clove garlic, minced

- 2 cups baby spinach

- ¼ cup crumbled feta cheese

Instructions:

- Preheat oven to 400°F.

- Prick sweet potatoes with a fork and place on a baking sheet. Bake for 40 minutes, until tender.

- Meanwhile, heat olive oil in a large skillet over medium heat.

- Add chickpeas, garlic, salt, and pepper and cook for 5 minutes, stirring occasionally.

- Add spinach and cook for 2 minutes, stirring occasionally.

- Cut sweet potatoes in half and top with chickpea mixture.

- Sprinkle with feta cheese and serve.

Prep Time: 45 minutes

7. Turkey and Black Bean Stuffed Peppers:

Ingredients:

- 4 red bell peppers

- 1 tablespoon olive oil

- 1 lb. ground turkey

- 1 teaspoon chili powder

- ½ teaspoon ground cumin

- ½ teaspoon garlic powder

- ½ teaspoon onion powder

- ½ teaspoon salt

- ½ teaspoon ground black pepper

- 1 (15 oz.) can black beans, drained and rinsed

- 1 cup cooked brown rice

- 1 cup salsa

- ½ cup shredded cheddar cheese

Instructions:

- Preheat oven to 375°F.

- Cut bell peppers in half lengthwise and remove seeds.

- Place peppers in a baking dish.

- Heat olive oil in a large skillet over medium heat.

- Add turkey and cook for 5 minutes, stirring occasionally and breaking up with a spoon.

- Add chili powder, cumin, garlic powder, onion powder, salt, and pepper and cook for 5 minutes, stirring occasionally.

- Add black beans, brown rice, and salsa and cook for 5 minutes, stirring occasionally.

- Spoon mixture into bell pepper halves.

- Top with shredded cheese and bake for 15 minutes, until cheese is melted and peppers are tender.

Prep Time: 30 minutes

8. Baked Salmon with Avocado Salsa:

Ingredients:

- 4 (4 oz.) salmon fillets

- 2 tablespoons olive oil

- ½ teaspoon salt

- ½ teaspoon ground black pepper

- 1 avocado, diced

- 1 tomato, diced

- ¼ cup diced red onion

- 2 tablespoons chopped fresh cilantro

- 2 tablespoons lime juice

Instructions:

- Preheat oven to 400°F.

- Brush salmon fillets with olive oil and season with salt and pepper.

- Place on a baking sheet and bake for 12 minutes, until cooked through.

- Meanwhile, in a small bowl, combine avocado, tomato, red onion, cilantro, and lime juice.

- Serve salmon with avocado salsa.

Prep Time: 15 minutes

9. Vegetarian Chili:

Ingredients:

- 1 tablespoon olive oil

- 1 onion, chopped

- 2 cloves garlic, minced

- 2 carrots, diced

- 2 stalks celery, diced

- 1 red bell pepper, chopped

- 1 green bell pepper, chopped

- 2 (15 oz.) cans black beans, drained and rinsed.

- 1 (14.5 oz.) can diced tomatoes

- 1 (8 oz.) can tomato sauce

- 2 tablespoons chili powder

- 1 teaspoon ground cumin

- ½ teaspoon salt

- ½ teaspoon ground black pepper

- 1 cup frozen corn

- 2 tablespoons chopped fresh parsley

Instructions:

- Heat olive oil in a large pot over medium heat.

- Add onion, garlic, carrots, celery, and bell peppers and cook for 5 minutes, stirring occasionally.

- Add black beans, diced tomatoes, tomato sauce, chili powder, cumin, salt, and pepper and bring to a boil.

- Reduce heat to low, cover, and simmer for 20 minutes, stirring occasionally.

- Stir in corn and cook for 5 minutes, stirring occasionally.

- Serve with chopped parsley.

Prep Time: 30 minutes

10. Mediterranean Quinoa Salad:

Ingredients:

- 1 cup uncooked quinoa

- 2 cups vegetable broth

- 1 (15 oz.) can chickpeas, drained and rinsed

- 1 cup diced cucumber

- ½ cup diced red onion

- ½ cup crumbled feta cheese

- ¼ cup chopped fresh parsley

- 2 tablespoons olive oil

- 2 tablespoons red wine vinegar

- 1 teaspoon dried oregano

- ½ teaspoon salt

- ½ teaspoon ground black pepper

Instructions:

- In a medium saucepan, combine quinoa and vegetable broth. Bring to a boil. Reduce heat to low, cover, and simmer for 15 minutes.

- In a large bowl, combine cooked quinoa, chickpeas, cucumber, red onion, feta cheese, and parsley.

- In a small bowl, whisk together olive oil, red wine vinegar, oregano, salt, and pepper.

- Pour dressing over quinoa mixture and toss to combine.

- Serve chilled or at room temperature.

Prep Time: 25 minutes

Snacks
20 snacks recipes with ingredients and instructions with prep time

1. Peanut Butter and Jelly Oatmeal Bars – Prep Time: 10 minutes

Ingredients:

2 cups rolled oats

2 tablespoons peanut butter

1/4 cup honey

1/4 cup jelly

Instructions:

1. Preheat oven to 350°F.

2. In a medium bowl, mix together the oats, peanut butter, honey, and jelly until combined.

3. Grease an 8x8 inch baking pan.

4. Spread the mixture into the pan and press down firmly.

5. Bake for 20 minutes or until golden brown.

6. Allow to cool before cutting into bars. Enjoy!

2. Yogurt Fruit Dip – Prep Time: 10 minutes

Ingredients:

1 cup plain Greek yogurt

2 tablespoons honey

1 teaspoon vanilla extract

Instructions:

1. In a medium bowl, mix together the yogurt, honey, and vanilla extract until smooth.

2. Serve with fresh fruit of your choice. Enjoy!

3. Caramel Popcorn – Prep Time: 10 minutes

Ingredients:

3 tablespoons butter

3 tablespoons brown sugar

1/4 teaspoon salt

1/4 teaspoon baking soda

4 cups popped popcorn

Instructions:

1. Preheat oven to 250°F.

2. In a small saucepan over medium heat, melt butter and brown sugar. Stir continuously until mixture comes to a boil.

3. Remove from heat and stir in salt and baking soda.

4. In a large bowl, combine popcorn and caramel mixture. Toss until popcorn is evenly coated.

5. Spread popcorn onto a baking sheet lined with parchment paper.

6. Bake for 25 minutes, stirring every 10 minutes.

7. Allow to cool before serving. Enjoy!

4. Chocolate Chip Cookies – Prep Time: 10 minutes

Ingredients:

1/2 cup butter, softened

1/2 cup granulated sugar

1/2 cup light brown sugar

1 egg

1 teaspoon vanilla extract

1 1/2 cups all-purpose flour

1/2 teaspoon baking soda

1/2 teaspoon salt

1 cup semi-sweet chocolate chips

Instructions:

1. Preheat oven to 350°F.

2. In a large bowl, cream together butter and sugars until light and fluffy.

3. Beat in egg and vanilla extract.

4. In a separate bowl, whisk together flour, baking soda, and salt.

5. Slowly add dry ingredients to wet ingredients, stirring until just combined.

6. Fold in chocolate chips.

7. Drop by tablespoonfuls onto baking sheets lined with parchment paper.

8. Bake for 8-10 minutes or until lightly golden brown.

9. Allow to cool before serving. Enjoy!

5. Baked Apple Chips – Prep Time: 10 minutes

Ingredients:

2 large apples

1 teaspoon ground cinnamon

2 tablespoons sugar

Instructions:

1. Preheat oven to 200°F.

2. Line two baking sheets with parchment paper.

3. Slice apples into thin slices, about 1/8 inch thick.

4. Place apple slices onto prepared baking sheets.

5. Sprinkle with cinnamon and sugar.

6. Bake for 1 1/2 hours or until chips are crisp.

7. Allow to cool before serving. Enjoy!

6. Peanut Butter Banana Bites – Prep Time: 10 minutes

Ingredients:

2 large bananas

2 tablespoons peanut butter

2 tablespoons mini chocolate chips

Instructions:

1. Slice each banana into 4 even slices.

2. Spread each slice with peanut butter.

3. Sprinkle with mini chocolate chips.

4. Serve immediately or store in an airtight container in the refrigerator for up to 2 days. Enjoy!

7. Tortilla Pizza Bites – Prep Time: 10 minutes

Ingredients:

4 flour tortillas

1/2 cup pizza sauce

1 cup shredded mozzarella cheese

1/2 cup grated Parmesan cheese

Instructions:

1. Preheat oven to 400°F.

2. Place tortillas on a baking sheet lined with parchment paper.

3. Spread each tortilla with pizza sauce.

4. Top with mozzarella and Parmesan cheese.

5. Bake for 8-10 minutes or until cheese is melted and bubbly.

6. Cut into wedges and serve. Enjoy!

8. Bacon Wrapped Potato Bites – Prep Time: 10 minutes

Ingredients:

8 small potatoes

4 slices bacon

1 tablespoon olive oil

Salt and pepper to taste

Instructions:

1. Preheat oven to 400°F.

2. Cut potatoes into 1 inch cubes.

3. Wrap each cube with bacon and secure with a toothpick.

4. Place on a baking sheet lined with parchment paper and brush with olive oil.

5. Sprinkle with salt and pepper.

6. Bake for 20 minutes or until bacon is crisp.

7. Allow to cool before serving. Enjoy!

9. Zucchini Fritters – Prep Time: 10 minutes

Ingredients:

2 cups shredded zucchini

1/4 cup all-purpose flour

1/4 cup grated Parmesan cheese

1/2 teaspoon garlic powder

1/2 teaspoon onion powder

Salt and pepper to taste

Instructions:

1. In a medium bowl, mix together zucchini, flour, Parmesan cheese, garlic powder, onion powder, salt and pepper until combined.

2. Form mixture into small patties.

3. Heat a large skillet over medium heat and add a tablespoon of oil.

4. Add patties to skillet and cook for 2-3 minutes per side or until golden brown.

5. Serve with your favorite dipping sauce. Enjoy!

10. Baked Carrot Fries – Prep Time: 10 minutes

Ingredients:

4 large carrots, peeled and cut into fries

1 tablespoon olive oil

Salt and pepper to taste

Instructions:

1. Preheat oven to 400°F.

2. Place carrots on a baking sheet lined with parchment paper and drizzle with olive oil.

3. Sprinkle with salt and pepper.

4. Bake for 20 minutes or until golden brown.

5. Serve with your favorite dipping sauce. Enjoy!

Desserts
10 desserts recipes with ingredients and instructions with prep time

1. Chocolate Chip Cookies

Ingredients:

- 2 and 1/4 cups all-purpose flour

- 1 teaspoon baking soda

- 1 teaspoon salt

- 1 cup (2 sticks) butter, softened

- 3/4 cup granulated sugar

- 3/4 cup packed brown sugar

- 1 teaspoon vanilla extract

- 2 large eggs

- 2 cups (12-oz. pkg.) semisweet chocolate chips

Instructions:

Preheat oven to 375°F.

In medium bowl, combine flour, baking soda and salt; set aside.

In large bowl, beat butter, granulated sugar, brown sugar and vanilla extract with electric mixer on medium speed until creamy. Add eggs, one at a time, beating well after each addition. Gradually beat in flour mixture. Stir in chocolate chips.

Drop dough by rounded tablespoonful onto ungreased baking sheets.

Bake 8 to 10 minutes or until golden brown. Cool on baking sheets 2 minutes; remove to wire racks to cool completely.

Prep Time: 15 minutes | Cook Time: 10 minutes

2. Apple Pie

Ingredients:

- 2 refrigerated pie crusts

- 4 Granny Smith apples, peeled, cored and thinly sliced

- 1/2 cup sugar

- 2 tablespoons all-purpose flour

- 1 teaspoon ground cinnamon

- 1/4 teaspoon ground nutmeg

- 2 tablespoons butter

- 2 tablespoons heavy cream

Instructions:

Preheat oven to 425°F.

In a large bowl, combine apples, sugar, flour, cinnamon and nutmeg; mix well.

Roll out one pie crust and place in 9-inch pie plate. Pour apple mixture into pie plate and dot with butter.

Roll out remaining pie crust and place over apple mixture. Cut off excess dough and pinch edges together. Cut 4 to 5 slits in top of crust. Brush top crust with cream.

Bake in preheated oven for 40 to 50 minutes, or until crust is golden brown. Allow to cool before serving.

Prep Time: 30 minutes | Cook Time: 40-50 minutes

3. Carrot Cake

Ingredients:

- 2 cups all-purpose flour

- 2 teaspoons baking powder

- 1 teaspoon baking soda

- 1 teaspoon ground cinnamon

- 1/2 teaspoon ground nutmeg

- 1/2 teaspoon salt

- 1/2 cup vegetable oil

- 1/2 cup buttermilk

- 1/2 cup packed light brown sugar

- 1/2 cup granulated sugar

- 3 large eggs

- 2 cups grated carrots

- 1 cup chopped walnuts

- 1 teaspoon vanilla extract

Instructions:

Preheat oven to 350°F. Grease and flour a 9x13-inch baking pan.

In a medium bowl, combine flour, baking powder, baking soda, cinnamon, nutmeg and salt; mix well.

In a large bowl, combine oil, buttermilk, sugars, eggs, carrots, walnuts and vanilla extract; mix until combined. Add flour mixture and stir until just combined.

Pour batter into prepared pan and bake in preheated oven for 25 to 30 minutes, or until a toothpick inserted in center comes out clean. Allow to cool before serving.

Prep Time: 20 minutes | Cook Time: 25-30 minutes

4. Banana Split Cake

Ingredients:

- 1 box white cake mix

- 2 (3.4-oz.) packages instant banana pudding

- 1 (20-oz.) can crushed pineapple, undrained

- 2 cups sliced fresh strawberries

- 1 (8-oz.) container frozen whipped topping, thawed

- 2 tablespoons chopped walnuts

- 2 bananas, sliced

Instructions:

Preheat oven to 350°F. Grease a 9x13-inch baking pan.

Prepare cake mix according to package instructions and pour into prepared pan. Bake in preheated oven for 25 to 30 minutes, or until a toothpick inserted in center comes out clean. Cool completely.

In a medium bowl, combine pudding mixes and pineapple. Spread over cooled cake. Top with strawberries, whipped topping and walnuts. Arrange banana slices on top.

Refrigerate until ready to serve.

Prep Time: 20 minutes | Cook Time: 25-30 minutes

5. Strawberry Shortcake

Ingredients:

- 2 cups all-purpose flour

- 2 tablespoons sugar

- 1 tablespoon baking powder

- 1/2 teaspoon salt

- 1/2 cup (1 stick) butter, melted

- 3/4 cup milk

- 2 cups sliced fresh strawberries

- 1/2 cup heavy cream

- 2 tablespoons powdered sugar

Instructions:

Preheat oven to 375°F. Grease a 9-inch round cake pan.

In a large bowl, combine flour, sugar, baking powder and salt. Add butter and milk; stir until just combined. Spread batter into prepared pan.

Bake in preheated oven for 25 to 30 minutes, or until a toothpick inserted in center comes out clean. Cool completely.

In a medium bowl, combine strawberries and cream. Beat with electric mixer on medium-high speed until stiff peaks form. Add powdered sugar; beat until combined.

Slice shortcake in half and spread with strawberry cream. Top with remaining shortcake and serve.

Prep Time: 20 minutes | Cook Time: 25-30 minutes

6. Chocolate Mousse

Ingredients:

- 4 (1-oz.) squares semi-sweet chocolate

- 2 tablespoons butter

- 2 tablespoons hot water

- 1 teaspoon vanilla extract

- 4 eggs, separated

- 1/4 teaspoon cream of tartar

- 1/4 cup granulated sugar

Instructions:

Melt chocolate and butter in a double boiler over low heat, stirring until smooth. Remove from heat and stir in hot water and vanilla extract.

In a medium bowl, beat egg whites and cream of tartar with electric mixer on medium speed until foamy. Gradually add sugar, 1 tablespoon at a time, beating until stiff peaks form.

In a separate bowl, beat egg yolks until light and fluffy. Gradually add melted chocolate mixture, beating until combined.

Gently fold egg whites into chocolate mixture. Spoon into 6 individual serving dishes and refrigerate for at least 2 hours.

Prep Time: 10 minutes | Refrigerate Time: 2 hours

7. Apple Crisp

Ingredients:

- 6 cups thinly sliced apples

- 1 cup packed brown sugar

- 1/2 cup all-purpose flour

- 1 teaspoon ground cinnamon

- 1/4 teaspoon ground nutmeg

- 1/4 teaspoon salt

- 1/2 cup (1 stick) butter, melted

- 1 cup quick-cooking oats

Instructions:

Preheat oven to 375°F. Grease an 8x8-inch baking dish.

In a large bowl, combine apples, brown sugar, flour, cinnamon, nutmeg and salt; mix well. Spoon into prepared baking dish.

In a medium bowl, combine butter and oats; mix well. Sprinkle over apple mixture.

Bake in preheated oven for 30 to 35 minutes, or until apples are tender and topping is golden brown. Serve warm.

Prep Time: 10 minutes | Cook Time: 30-35 minutes

8. Brownies

Ingredients:

- 2/3 cup all-purpose flour

- 1/4 teaspoon salt

- 1/4 teaspoon baking powder

- 4 (1-oz.) squares unsweetened chocolate

- 1/2 cup (1 stick) butter

- 1 cup granulated sugar

- 2 large eggs

- 1 teaspoon vanilla extract

Instructions:

Preheat oven to 350°F. Grease an 8x8-inch baking pan.

In a small bowl, combine flour, salt and baking powder; set aside.

Melt chocolate and butter in a double boiler over low heat, stirring until smooth. Remove from heat and stir in sugar. Add eggs, one at a time, stirring well after each addition. Stir in vanilla extract. Gradually add flour mixture, stirring until combined.

Pour batter into prepared pan and bake in preheated oven for 25 to 30 minutes, or until a toothpick inserted in center comes out clean. Cool before cutting into bars.

Prep Time: 10 minutes | Cook Time: 25-30 minutes

9. Cheesecake

Ingredients:

- 2 (8-oz.) packages cream cheese, softened

- 1/2 cup sugar

- 2 large eggs

- 1 teaspoon vanilla extract

- 1 (9-inch) graham cracker crust

- 1/2 cup sour cream

Instructions:

Preheat oven to 350°F.

In a large bowl, beat cream cheese and sugar with electric mixer on medium speed until light and fluffy. Add eggs, one at a time, beating well after each addition. Stir in vanilla extract. Pour into prepared crust.

Bake in preheated oven for 30 minutes. Remove from oven and spread sour cream over top. Return to oven and bake an additional 10 minutes. Cool completely before serving.

Prep Time: 20 minutes | Cook Time: 40 minutes

10. Baked Donuts

Ingredients:

- 2 cups all-purpose flour

- 1/2 cup sugar

- 1 tablespoon baking powder

- 1/2 teaspoon salt

- 3/4 cup milk

- 2 eggs

- 4 tablespoons butter, melted

- 2 teaspoons vanilla extract

- 1/4 teaspoon ground nutmeg

- 1/4 cup melted butter

- 1/2 cup sugar

Instructions:

Preheat oven to 425°F. Grease a donut pan.

In a large bowl, combine flour, sugar, baking powder, salt, milk, eggs, melted butter, vanilla extract and nutmeg; mix until just combined.

Fill donut pan with batter, filling each cavity about 3/4 full. Bake in preheated oven for 8 to 10 minutes, or until golden brown.

Remove from oven and brush with melted butter. Dip in sugar to coat. Serve warm.

Prep Time: 15 minutes | Cook Time: 8-10 minutes

CHAPTER FIVE
Meal Planning

1. Decide on a weekly budget: Before you start meal planning, determine what you have to spend on groceries each week. This will allow you to plan meals that are within your budget.

2. Gather recipes: Look through cookbooks, magazines, and online resources to find recipes that you and your family can enjoy. Make sure to consider dietary restrictions and food allergies when selecting recipes.

3. Make a grocery list: Based on the recipes you have chosen, make a list of the ingredients that you need to buy. Be sure to check your cupboards and refrigerator for items that you already have.

4. Plan your meals: Once you have your recipes and grocery list, decide what meals you will make each day. Make sure to include a variety of proteins, fruits, vegetables, and whole grains.

5. Shop for groceries: Take your grocery list and head to the store. Be sure to check prices and look for sales and coupons to help you stay within your budget.

6. Prepare food: Once you have all of your groceries, take time to prepare food for the week. Wash fruits and vegetables, cook proteins, and prepare meals ahead of time.

7. Pack lunches: If you or your family members are taking lunch to work or school, plan ahead and make sure to pack healthy options.

8. Store food: Make sure to store food properly to prevent spoilage. Label containers and use airtight containers to keep food fresh.

9. Reheat meals: Reheating leftovers is an easy way to save time and money. Make sure to reheat food to the correct temperature to avoid food poisoning.

10. Enjoy meals: Finally, sit down and enjoy your meal. Eating together can strengthen family bonds and promote healthy eating habits.

CHAPTER SIX
Healthy Eating Tips

1. Eat a variety of foods. Eating a variety of foods will ensure you get all the essential vitamins, minerals, and other nutrients your body needs.

2. Make half of your plate fruits and vegetables. Eating a variety of fruits and vegetables will ensure you get all the vitamins, minerals, and other nutrients your body needs.

3. Choose whole grain foods. Whole grains are an excellent source of fiber and other important vitamins and minerals.

4. Choose lean proteins. Lean proteins, such as fish, chicken, and beans, provide your body with essential amino acids.

5. Limit added sugar. Added sugar can increase your risk of obesity, heart disease, and other health problems.

6. Limit processed and refined foods. Processed and refined foods are often high in unhealthy fats, sugar, and sodium.

7. Eat fewer saturated fats. Saturated fats, such as those found in butter and red meat, can increase your risk of heart disease.

8. Eat more healthy fats. Healthy fats, such as those found in olive oil, avocado, and nuts, can help lower your cholesterol.

9. Eat more plant-based proteins. Plant-based proteins, such as beans, lentils, and nuts, are an excellent source of essential nutrients.

10. Eat fewer processed meats. Processed meats, such as hot dogs and bacon, are high in sodium and unhealthy fats.

11. Eat smaller portions. Eating smaller portions can help you control your calorie intake and maintain a healthy weight.

12. Choose low-fat dairy products. Low-fat dairy products, such as milk, yogurt, and cheese, are an excellent source of calcium and other essential nutrients.

13. Drink water instead of sugary drinks. Sugary drinks, such as soda and energy drinks, are high in calories and can increase your risk of obesity and other health problems.

14. Avoid skipping meals. Skipping meals can lead to unhealthy snacking and can cause your blood sugar levels to spike.

15. Limit alcohol consumption. Excessive alcohol consumption can increase your risk of liver disease and other health problems.

16. Eat more fiber. Fiber can help you feel full and can help lower your cholesterol.

17. Eat more seafood. Seafood, such as fish and shellfish, are an excellent source of protein and omega-3 fatty acids.

18. Read nutrition labels. Reading nutrition labels can help you make healthier food choices.

19. Plan your meals. Planning your meals ahead of time can help you make healthier food choices.

20. Get creative in the kitchen. Trying new recipes and ingredients can help you expand your meal options and try new flavors.

CHAPTER SEVEN
Food Safety

1. Store food at the right temperature: Hot foods should be kept at an internal temperature of 140°F or warmer and cold foods should be kept at 40°F or colder.

2. Separate foods: Raw foods should be stored separately from cooked foods to prevent cross-contamination.

3. Cook food to the right temperature: Meat, poultry, seafood, and eggs should be cooked to the right internal temperature to kill any bacteria or parasites that may be present.

4. Use clean utensils and equipment: Utensils and equipment should be cleaned and sanitized regularly to prevent the spread of bacteria.

5. Avoid cross-contamination: Use separate cutting boards for raw meat, poultry, and seafood to avoid cross-contamination.

6. Wash hands frequently: Hands should be washed thoroughly before, during, and after handling food to prevent the spread of bacteria.

7. Avoid raw foods: Uncooked eggs, milk, and meat should be avoided, as these foods may contain harmful bacteria.

8. Reheat food properly: Heated food should be reheated to an internal temperature of 165°F or higher to kill any bacteria that may have grown during storage.

9. Don't leave food out: Perishable foods should not be left out for more than two hours at room temperature.

10. Refrigerate leftovers: Leftover food should be refrigerated within two hours of cooking to prevent the growth of bacteria.

11. Use clean dishes: Dishes should be washed with hot, soapy water before and after use to prevent the spread of bacteria.

12. Use pasteurized dairy products: Dairy products should be pasteurized to kill any harmful bacteria that may be present.

13. Use clean water: Water used for cooking and drinking should be clean and free of contaminants.

14. Avoid canned foods with dents or bulging lids: Canned foods with dents or bulging lids may be contaminated with harmful bacteria.

15. Avoid expired foods: Foods that have passed their expiration date should be discarded to prevent contamination.

16. Clean produce: Fruits and vegetables should be washed before consuming to remove any dirt or bacteria present.

17. Avoid food from unlicensed vendors: Food from unlicensed vendors may contain harmful bacteria and should be avoided.

18. Follow food handling instructions: Instructions for food handling should be followed to prevent the spread of bacteria.

19. Get vaccinated: Vaccines are available that can help protect against food-borne illnesses such as salmonella and E. coli.

20. Learn food safety: Knowing the basics of food safety is essential for preventing food-borne illnesses.

CHAPTER EIGHT
Cooking Methods

1. Baking: Baking is a cooking method that involves the dry heat of an oven. Foods that are baked can include cakes, pies, cookies, breads, and pastries.

2. Boiling: Boiling is a cooking method that involves submerging food in boiling water or other liquid. Foods that are boiled can include vegetables, pasta, rice, and eggs.

3. Broiling: Broiling is a cooking method that involves placing food under direct heat. Foods that are broiled can include meats, fish, and vegetables.

4. Grilling: Grilling is a cooking method that involves cooking food over direct heat from below. Foods that are grilled can include meats, fish, and vegetables.

5. Frying: Frying is a cooking method that involves cooking food in hot oil or fat. Foods that are fried can include meats, fish, and vegetables.

6. Roasting: Roasting is a cooking method that involves cooking food in an oven or over an open fire. Foods that are roasted can include meats, fish, and vegetables.

7. Sautéing: Sautéing is a cooking method that involves cooking food in a small amount of fat over direct heat. Foods that are sautéed can include meats, fish, and vegetables.

8. Steaming: Steaming is a cooking method that involves cooking food by exposing it to steam. Foods that are steamed can include vegetables, fish, and dumplings.

9. Poaching: Poaching is a cooking method that involves cooking food in a liquid such as water, milk, or stock. Foods that are poached can include eggs, fish, and poultry.

10. Simmering: Simmering is a cooking method that involves cooking food in liquid at just below the boiling point. Foods that are simmered can include soups, stews, and sauces.

11. Braising: Braising is a cooking method that involves cooking food in liquid over low heat. Foods that are braised can include meats and vegetables.

12. Stewing: Stewing is a cooking method that involves cooking food in liquid over low heat for a long period of time. Foods that are stewed can include meats, vegetables, and beans.

13. Pressure Cooking: Pressure cooking is a cooking method that involves cooking food in steam under pressure. Foods that are pressure cooked can include meats, fish, and vegetables.

14. Stir-Frying: Stir-frying is a cooking method that involves cooking food in a small amount of fat over high heat. Foods that are stir-fried can include meats, fish, and vegetables.

15. Blanching: Blanching is a cooking method that involves immersing food in boiling water for a brief period of time. Foods that are blanched can include vegetables, fruits, and nuts.

16. Deep-Frying: Deep-frying is a cooking method that involves cooking food in hot oil or fat. Foods that are deep-fried can include meats, fish, and vegetables.

17. Microwaving: Microwaving is a cooking method that involves cooking food with microwave radiation. Foods that are microwaved can include meats, fish, and vegetables.

18. Marinating: Marinating is a cooking method that involves soaking food in a marinade. Foods that are marinated can include meats, fish, and vegetables.

19. Stuffing: Stuffing is a cooking method that involves filling a food with a savory mixture. Foods that are stuffed can include meats, vegetables, and fruits.

20. Smoking: Smoking is a cooking method that involves exposing food to smoke from burning wood chips or other materials. Foods that are smoked can include meats, fish, and vegetables.

CHAPTER NINE
Cooking Tips

1. Use sharp knives and other kitchen tools. Dull knives and other tools make it more difficult to prepare food and can increase the risk of injury.

2. Make sure to read recipes thoroughly before beginning. This will help you become familiar with the ingredients and the steps required to complete the recipe.

3. Prepare all ingredients before beginning. This will help you move quickly and efficiently while cooking.

4. Use a timer when cooking. This will help you keep track of how long food has been cooking and will prevent overcooking.

5. Taste food as you cook. This will help you adjust seasoning and cooking times to ensure the best results.

6. Use the right pan for the job. Different types of pans are best for different types of cooking.

7. Keep a clean workspace. This will make it easier to prepare food and will reduce the risk of cross-contamination.

8. Heat oil in a pan before adding food. This will help the food cook evenly and reduce the chance of it sticking to the pan.

9. Use fresh ingredients whenever possible. Fresh ingredients often have more flavor than their canned or frozen counterparts.

10. Measure ingredients accurately. This will help ensure the flavors of the dish are balanced and the texture is as desired.

11. Use herbs and spices to add flavor. Herbs and spices can add depth and complexity to dishes.

12. Cook food to the proper temperature. This will ensure food is cooked through and safe to eat.

13. Use a thermometer when necessary. This will help you ensure the food is cooked to the proper temperature.

14. Let food rest before serving. This will help the flavors develop and will allow the food to cool down.

15. Use the right cooking techniques. Different cooking techniques can drastically affect the flavor and texture of food.

16. Be creative. Try adding new flavors and ingredients to dishes to make them more interesting.

17. Keep kitchen appliances clean. Dirty appliances can harbor bacteria and can make food taste bad.

18. Store food properly. Proper storage will help ensure food stays fresh and safe to eat.

19. Be mindful of food safety. Follow food safety guidelines to prevent foodborne illnesses.

20. Have fun! Cooking should be enjoyable and a chance to express yourself in the kitchen.

Conclusion

Cooking solo can be a fantastic and fulfilling experience. Not only is it a great way to save money and time, but it can also be a great way to learn about yourself and develop your cooking skills. By taking the time to plan, shop, and prepare your own meals, you can learn how to cook interesting and nutritious dishes that you may not have had the opportunity to try otherwise. Additionally, it can be a wonderful way to relax and enjoy the process of creating something delicious. With a little bit of effort and imagination, cooking solo can be a rewarding and enjoyable experience. So, don't be afraid to step out of your comfort zone and give cooking solo a try. With a few simple tips, you can turn your kitchen into a place of exploration and delight. With a little effort, you can transform the ordinary into something extraordinary. So, why not take the plunge and start cooking solo today? You'll be glad you did. Thank you for taking the time to read about cooking solo. We hope this book has inspired you to give it a try and to discover the joy of creating something delicious all on your own. Bon appétit!